T0268544

CAMBRIDGE
UNIVERSITY PRESS

Click Start

INTERNATIONAL EDITION

Learner's Book 2

CAMBRIDGE
UNIVERSITY PRESS

University Printing House, Cambridge CB2 8BS, United Kingdom

One Liberty Plaza, 20th Floor, New York, NY 10006, USA

477 Williamstown Road, Port Melbourne, VIC 3207, Australia

314–321, 3rd Floor, Plot 3, Splendor Forum, Jasola District Centre, New Delhi – 110025, India

79 Anson Road, #06–04/06, Singapore 079906

Cambridge University Press is part of the University of Cambridge.

It furthers the University's mission by disseminating knowledge in the pursuit of
education, learning and research at the highest international levels of excellence.

www.cambridge.org
Information on this title: www.cambridge.org/9781108951821

© Cambridge University Press 2021

This publication is in copyright. Subject to statutory exception
and to the provisions of relevant collective licensing agreements,
no reproduction of any part may take place without the written
permission of Cambridge University Press.

First published 2021

20 19 18 17 16 15 14 13 12 11 10 9 8 7 6 5 4 3 2 1

Printed in Poland by Opolgraf

ISBN 978-1-108-95182-1 Paperback

Cambridge University Press has no responsibility for the persistence or accuracy
of URLs for external or third-party internet websites referred to in this publication,
and does not guarantee that any content on such websites is, or will remain,
accurate or appropriate. Information regarding prices, travel timetables, and other
factual information given in this work is correct at the time of first printing but
Cambridge University Press does not guarantee the accuracy of such information
thereafter.

....

NOTICE TO TEACHERS IN THE UK
It is illegal to reproduce any part of this work in material form (including
photocopying and electronic storage) except under the following circumstances:
(i)   where you are abiding by a licence granted to your school or institution by the
       Copyright Licensing Agency;
(ii)   where no such licence exists, or where you wish to exceed the terms of a licence,
       and you have gained the written permission of Cambridge University Press;
(iii) where you are allowed to reproduce without permission under the provisions
       of Chapter 3 of the Copyright, Designs and Patents Act 1988, which covers, for
       example, the reproduction of short passages within certain types of educational
       anthology and reproduction for the purposes of setting examination questions.

....

Every effort has been made to trace the owners of copyright material included in this
book. The publishers would be grateful for any omissions brought to their notice for
acknowledgement in future editions of the book.

Introduction

The international edition of ***Click Start: Computing for Schools*** is designed around the latest developments in the field of computer science, information and communication technology. Based on Windows 7 and MS Office 2010, with extensive updates on Windows 10 and MS Office 2016, the series aids the understanding of the essentials of computer science including computer basics, office applications, creative software, programming concepts and programming languages.

Each level of the series has been designed keeping in mind the learning ability of the learners as well as their interests. Efforts have been made to use examples from day-to-day life, which will help the learners to bridge the gap between their knowledge of the subject and the real world. The books are designed to offer a holistic approach and help in the overall development of the learners.

KEY FEATURES

- **Snap Recap:** Probing questions to begin a chapter and assess pre-knowledge
- **Learning Objectives:** A list of the learning outcomes of the chapter
- **Activity:** Interactive exercise after every major topic to reinforce analytical skills and application-based learning
- **Exercise:** A variety of questions to test understanding
- **Fact File:** Interesting concept-related snippets to improve concept knowledge
- **Quick Key** and **Try This:** Shortcuts and useful tips on options available for different operations
- **Glossary:** Chapter-end list of important terms along with their definitions
- **You Are Here:** Quick recap
- **Lab Work:** Practical exercises to enable application of concepts through learning-by-doing
- **Project Work:** Situational tasks to test practical application of the concepts learnt
- **Who Am I?:** Biographies to inspire young learners
- **Sample Paper:** Practice and preparation for exams

The books, thus, will not only make learning fun but also help the learners achieve a certain level of expertise in this fast changing world of computer science.

Overview

Snap Recap
Probing questions to begin a chapter and assess pre-knowledge

SNAP RECAP

A computer has 4 basic parts which are:
....
....
....
....

Learning Objectives
A list of the learning outcomes of the chapter

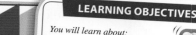

LEARNING OBJECTIVES

You will learn about:
- input devices
- processing device
- output devices
- storage devices

Activity
Interactive exercises after every major topic to reinforce analytical skills and application-based learning

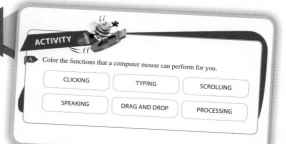

ACTIVITY

A. Color the functions that a computer mouse can perform for you.

| CLICKING | TYPING | SCROLLING |
| SPEAKING | DRAG AND DROP | PROCESSING |

Exercise
A variety of questions to test understanding

EXERCISE

A. State true or false.
1. Devices that help us enter data into the computer are called output devices.
2. We can give input to a computer with the help of a mouse.
3. A microphone makes computer games a lot more fun.
4. A scanner is used to take live photos and videos.
5. The full form of CPU is Computer Programming Unit.
6. A printer prints the results of your work from the computer screen on a sheet of paper.

FACT FILE

Web-call can be made using computer and the Internet.

Fact File
Interesting concept-related snippets to improve concept knowledge

Quick Key and **Try This**
Shortcuts and useful tips on options available for different operations

TRY THIS

Press **Ctrl + N** to open a new document.

Glossary
Chapter-end list of important terms along with their definitions

GLOSSARY

Double-clicking It is the pressing of the left mouse button twice within a short interval of time.
Icon It is a small picture-like item on a computer screen (desktop) that you click on to open an application.
Operating system It controls how different parts of a computer work together.
Start button It is used for opening programs, applications and documents, changing settings and shutting down the computer.
Taskbar It is the blue bar at the bottom of the desktop.
Windows It is an operating system.

You Are Here
Summary for a quick recap

YOU ARE HERE 2
1. Starting the computer:
Switch on the power button ➡ Switch on the UPS ➡ Switch on the CPU ➡ Switch on the monitor
2. Windows is an operating system that runs your computer.
3. The desktop is the display screen that appears once the computer is switched on.
4. Taskbar displays the opened applications.
5. Shutting down the computer:
Click on the Start button ➡ Click on the Shut down option ➡ Switch off the monitor ➡ Switch off the UPS ➡ Switch off the power button.

Lab Work
Practical exercises to enable application of concepts through learning-by-doing

LAB WORK
A. Use post-it slips and label the different input and output devices on your computer.
B. Insert/Connect a CD/pen drive in the computer system and tell what happens when you do this.

Project Work
Situational tasks to test practical application of the concepts learnt

PROJECT WORK
Interview 5 people (parents, siblings, grandparents, friends and neighbours) around you to find out what do they use a computer for. Now, collate the list with members of your group to make a sheet about uses of computer.

Sample Paper
Helps test learner understanding at the end of the course

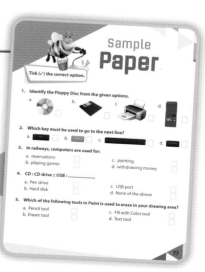

Sample **Paper**

Tick (✓) the correct option.

1. Identify the Floppy Disc from the given options.
   a.   b.   c.   d.

2. Which key must be used to go to the next line?
   a.   b.   c.   d.

3. In railways, computers are used for:
   a. reservations
   b. playing games
   c. painting
   d. withdrawing money

4. CD : CD drive :: USB : ....
   a. Pen drive
   b. Hard disk
   c. USB port
   d. None of the above

5. Which of the following tools in Paint is used to erase in your drawing area?
   a. Pencil tool
   b. Eraser tool
   c. Fill with Color tool
   d. Text tool

77

Who Am I?
Biographies to inspire young learners

WHO AM I?
I was born on 14 February 1819.
I am the co-inventor of the typewriter.
I designed the arrangement of characters on a QWERTY keyboard in 1868.
I am ....

C🌐ntents ▶▶

Know Your Computer

SNAP RECAP

A computer has 4 basic parts which are:

....
....
....
....

LEARNING OBJECTIVES

You will learn about:
- input devices
- the processing device
- output devices
- storage devices

A computer is an electronic machine. It accepts data as input, processes it and gives information as output.

A computer works very fast. It saves you time and energy. A computer does not make mistakes on its own. It can remember a lot of things. The basic parts of a computer are shown in the picture given here. These parts of the computer and some other devices are connected by wires.

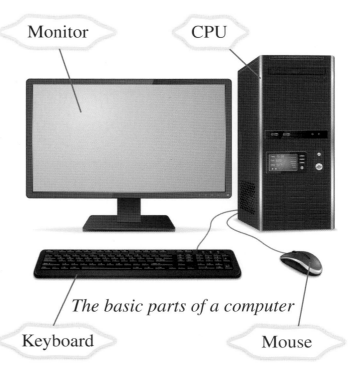

Monitor   CPU

Keyboard   Mouse

The basic parts of a computer

FACT FILE

There are also wireless mice and keyboards.

The basic parts of a computer system are:

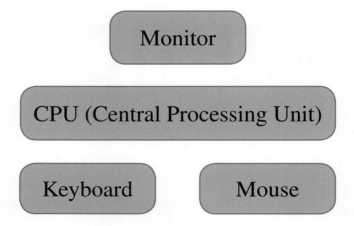

You will learn about these devices in detail and other devices that can be connected to a computer.

Input devices

Devices that help us enter data into the computer are called input devices. They help in giving instructions to the computer. You will now learn about these input devices.

Keyboard

A keyboard is used for entering data into the computer system. You can use it to type words, numbers and symbols.

Keyboard

Mouse

The mouse is a pointing device. You can give input/instructions to a computer using a mouse.

Mouse

Joystick

A joystick makes computer games a lot more fun. When it is moved, it passes information to the computer.

Joystick

Microphone

A microphone can be attached to a computer. It allows you to input sounds into the computer like speech and songs. You can record your voice with the help of a microphone. You can also use it for talking on a web-call.

Microphone

Web camera

A web camera is used to take live photos and videos. You can save them in the computer. You can also use a web camera for video streaming during a web-call.

Web camera

FACT FILE

Web-calls can be made using a computer and the Internet.

Scanner

A scanner copies pictures and pages, and turns them into images that can be saved on a computer.

Scanner

Processing device

All the inputs are stored, arranged and changed by a computer. The device that helps a computer to do this is called the processing device. The processing device in a computer is known as the **Central Processing Unit (CPU).** You might remember that the CPU is sometimes called the 'brain' of a computer.

CPU

Output devices

The parts of a computer that help us to show the results of processing are called output devices. You will now learn about these output devices.

Monitor

Monitor

A monitor looks like a TV screen. It shows whatever you type on the keyboard or draw with the mouse. A monitor can display both the input and the result of the processing.

Printer

A printer prints the result of your work from the computer screen on a sheet of paper. This is called a **printout**.

Printer

FACT FILE

The output as a printout is called a **hard copy**. The output displayed on the computer monitor is called a **soft copy**.

4

Speakers

Speakers

Speakers are the output devices that produce different types of sounds processed by a computer. You can listen to music or speeches stored in the computer using the speakers.

Headphones

You can listen to music or any sound from a computer with the help of headphones, without disturbing others. They are also helpful for listening during a web-call.

Headphones

Storage devices

The parts of a computer which are used for storing data are called storage devices. They help to permanently store any work done on a computer. You will now learn about different storage devices.

Hard disk

Hard disk

A hard disk is made up of one or more metallic disks. It stores a large amount of information.

Compact disc (CD)

A CD stores information. It is an external storage device which works when inserted into the CD drive. The CD drive is also fixed in the CPU.

CD

FACT FILE

Not handling the CD properly may result in loss of the data stored.

Pen drive

A pen drive is an external storage device that can store a large amount of data. It is also known as a flash drive. It can be easily carried around and works when inserted in the USB port found in the CPU of the computer.

The data stored in a pen drive can be removed, added and changed.

Pen drive

USB port in the CPU

TRY THIS

Find out how many USB ports there are in the CPU of your computer lab.

ACTIVITY

A. Look at the following pictures carefully. Color the boxes **red** if it is an input device, **blue** if it is an output device and **green** if it is a storage device.

B. Give one word for the following.

1. These help us to listen to music. ....
2. Looks like a TV screen. ....
3. A processing device. ....
4. A pointing device. ....
5. Used to make a printout. ....

GLOSSARY

Compact Disc (CD) An external storage device that stores information and works when inserted into a CD drive.

CPU The processing device in a computer.

Electronic machine A machine that runs with the help of electricity.

Hard disk A storage device that permanently stores a large amount of information.

Headphones The output device for listening to recorded sounds without disturbing others.

Input device A device that helps us enter data into the computer - for example, a keyboard.

Joystick An input device used for playing computer games.

Keyboard An input device used to enter data into the computer system.

Microphone An input device to send sounds into the computer.

Monitor An output device that shows whatever you type on the keyboard or draw with the mouse.

Mouse A pointing device.

Output device A device that helps us to show the input and result of processing.

Pen drive An external storage device that stores a large amount of data.

Processing device Helps to store, arrange and change the inputs on a computer.

Scanner Copies pictures and pages and turns them into images that can be saved on a computer.

Speakers An output device that is used for listening to recorded sound.

Storage device The parts of a computer that are used for storing data.

Web camera An input device used for taking live photos and videos.

1. Input devices help us to give instructions to the computer.
2. The keyboard, mouse, joystick, microphone, web camera and scanner are input devices.
3. The CPU (Central Processing Unit) is the processing device in a computer.
4. Output devices help us to show the result of processing done by the computer.
5. The monitor, printer, speakers and headphones are output devices.
6. Storage devices help us to permanently store any work we do on the computer.
7. The hard disk, compact disc (CD) and pen drive are storage devices.

EXERCISE

A. True or false?

1. Devices that help us enter data into the computer are called output devices.

2. We can give input to a computer with the help of a mouse.

3. A microphone makes computer games a lot more fun.

4. A scanner is used to take live photos and videos.

5. The full name of the CPU is Computer Programming Unit.

6. A printer prints the results of your work from the computer screen on a sheet of paper.

B. Circle the correct option.

1.

   Input/Output

2.

   Input/Output

3.

   Input/Output

4.

   Input/Output

C. Look at the pictures carefully. Identify the picture and fill in the missing letters.

1.  JOY ☐ TICK

2.  HEADPHO ☐ ES

3.  M ☐ CROPHONE

4.  WEB ☐ AMERA

5.  SCA ☐ NER

D. The clue given in each box has a partner. Match the pairs and color them alike.

1. MICROPHONE •   • a. DISPLAYS WHAT YOU TYPE

2. MONITOR •   • b. RECORDS SPEECH

3. PRINTER •   • c. STORES DATA

4. PEN DRIVE •   • d. GIVES PRINTOUT

E. Answer the following questions.

1. What is an input device?

   ....

2. List the four basic parts of computer system.

   ....

3. What is a processing device? Name the processing device in a computer.

   ....

   ....

4. Discuss and write about any two storage devices of a computer.

   ....

   ....

LAB WORK

A. Use post-it notes to label the different input and output devices on your computer.

B. Insert/connect a CD/pen drive in the computer system and find out what happens when you do this.

PROJECT WORK

Collect pictures of different input, processing and output devices. Bring them to the class and in groups of 4 make your own computer by choosing the devices. Label the various parts.

COMPUTER PARTS

monitor

CPU

speaker   printer

keyboard   mouse

WHO AM I?

I am known as the 'father of computers'.

I was born in the year 1791 in London.

I have created machines that could make tables and complete mathematical calculations faster than humans could.

I am ....

Working with Windows

SNAP RECAP

List a few things that we should be careful about when working on a computer.

....

....

LEARNING OBJECTIVES

You will learn about:
- starting a computer
- operating systems
- the desktop
- opening an application
- shutting down a computer

You have learned about the parts and functions of the computer. You will now learn how to start a computer. This chapter will discuss using Windows 7. For Windows 10 updates, go to the end of the chapter.

FACT FILE

Starting the computer system is also called booting the system.

Starting a computer

Write down the steps you need to follow when switching on a computer.

....

....

....

....

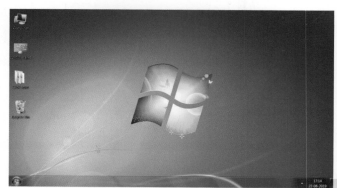

A Windows icon as shown here is seen when your computer is switched on.

Operating system

The operating system controls how different parts of a computer work together. Windows is an operating system that runs your computer. You can have different views from the windows of your house. In the same way, you can open and view many programs on your computer with the help of Windows.

Desktop

The desktop is the screen that appears once the computer is switched on. It is the display screen that has many small items on it. These are known as **icons**. An icon helps us to choose an item on the computer screen.

The Start button and the taskbar are located at the bottom of the desktop.

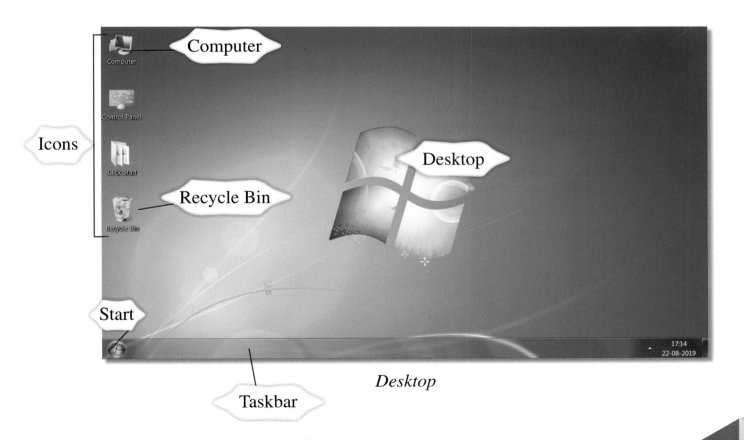

Desktop

Start

Start is a very important button. It is used for opening programs, applications and documents, changing settings, shutting down the computer and many other purposes.

FACT FILE

You can arrange the icons on your desktop by using the right click option on your mouse.

Taskbar

The taskbar is the bar at the bottom of the desktop. It shows the applications that you are currently using. It also allows you to quickly switch between them. It even displays the date and time.

Opening an application using the start menu

To open an application, for example, Calculator, you need to follow these steps:

1. Click on the **Start** button.
2. Click on **All Programs**.
3. Select **Accessories**. A list of options will appear.
4. Click on **Calculator**.

Opening Calculator using the Start menu

14

Once the **Calculator** window is open, it will appear as shown here.

Calculator window

The Close button is placed at the upper-right corner of the Calculator window. When you want to close this window, click on it.

Opening an application by selecting an icon on the desktop

1. Use the left click option on your mouse to click on any icon on the desktop.
2. When you click on the icon, the desktop area surrounding the icon gets highlighted.
3. To open the program, click the left mouse button twice very quickly. This is called **double-clicking**.

For example, by double-clicking the **Computer** icon on the desktop the following window is displayed.

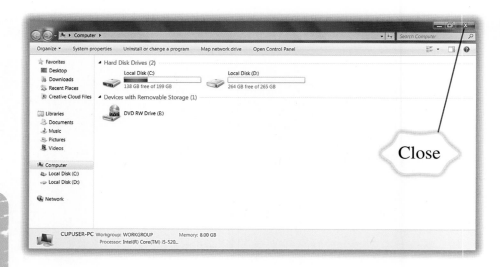

To close the Computer window, click on the 'X' button at the upper-right corner.

Shutting down a computer

Before shutting down your computer, close all the applications and windows. Then using the left-click on the mouse, click the Start button on your desktop. Now, look at the images below. Write the remaining steps to shut down your computer as shown in each image.

....

....

Never switch off the computer directly from the power button, CPU or UPS.

ACTIVITY

Find the following words in the grid below.

UPS		M	W	G	H	M	T	Y	F	R
WINDOWS		O	I	I	D	U	P	S	V	B
DESKTOP		N	N	T	Y	T	I	M	E	Y
ICONS		I	D	A	H	L	M	I	J	A
TASKBAR		T	O	S	B	M	Y	C	P	U
TIME		O	W	K	Z	C	S	L	N	A
CPU		R	S	B	X	R	D	I	D	G
MONITOR		R	T	A	G	Y	B	C	J	H
CLICK		W	E	R	Y	Q	U	K	I	O
		D	E	S	K	T	O	P	K	L
		H	J	K	I	C	O	N	S	P

GLOSSARY

Double-clicking Pressing the left mouse button twice very quickly.

Icon A small picture-like item on a computer screen (desktop) that you click on to open an application.

Operating system Controls how different parts of a computer work together.

Start button Used for opening programs, applications and documents, changing settings and shutting down the computer.

Taskbar The bar at the bottom of the desktop that shows the applications currently in use.

Windows An operating system.

YOU ARE
HERE

2

1. Starting the computer:

   Switch on the power button ⟹ Switch on the UPS ⟹ Switch on the CPU ⟹ Switch on the monitor

2. Windows is an operating system that runs your computer.

3. The desktop is the display screen that appears once the computer is switched on.

4. The taskbar displays the opened applications.

5. Shutting down the computer:

   Click on the Start button ⟹ Click on the Shut down option ⟹ Switch off the monitor ⟹ Switch off the UPS ⟹ Switch off the power button.

EXERCISE

A. Fill in the blanks with the correct word.

> desktop   icon   Double-clicking   bottom
> Start button   operating system

1. The .... controls how different parts of a computer work together.

2. .... is the pressing of the left mouse button twice very quickly.

3. A small picture-like item on a computer screen that you click on to open an application is called an ....

4. .... is used for opening programs, applications and documents, changing settings and turning off the computer.

5. The taskbar is the blue bar at the .... of the desktop.

6. A .... is the display screen that appears once the computer is switched on.

B. Match the following pairs.

1.	Windows	a.	Small picture-like items on the desktop
2.	Icons	b.	Consists of taskbar, icons and Start button
3.	Taskbar	c.	Used for opening programs
4.	Desktop	d.	Blue bar at the bottom of the desktop
5.	Start button	e.	Operating system

C. Label the following picture.

D. Based on the steps you learnt for opening the Calculator window, give the steps for opening the Paint window on your computer.

1. ....

2. ....

3. ....

4. ....

LAB WORK 🖥️

Switch on a computer. Try right-click and left-click on your mouse to explore various options of opening an application, closing an application and increasing/decreasing the size of icons.

PROJECT WORK

Find out information about the Windows 7 operating system. When was it released?

Is there any other latest version of Windows?

Windows 10
Updates

Windows 10 is the latest version of the Windows Operating System. It has a new Start screen. The Start screen has a Tile structure. You can browse through all the applications and open them. You can also search for applications in 'Type here to search' in the taskbar.

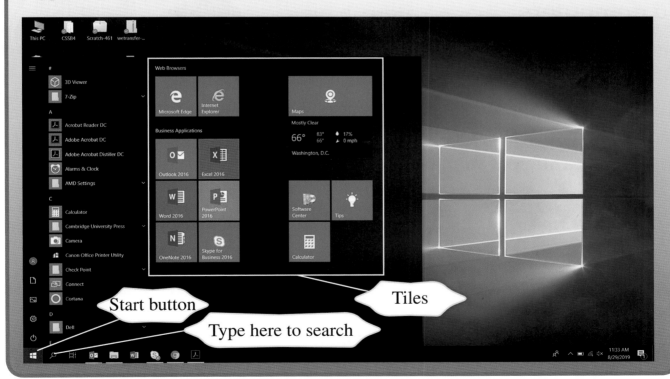

Start button

Tiles

Type here to search

Applications of a Computer

SNAP RECAP

List at least three machines. Explain how these machines are useful to us.

LEARNING OBJECTIVES

You will learn about:
*   humans and computers
*   types of computers
*   uses of computers

Differences between humans and computers

Humans have made a wonderful machine called the computer.

Computers make our work easier and also help us to do it faster. Let us find out how computers are different from humans.

Machines are made by humans

Speed

Computers work very fast.

Humans cannot work as fast as computers.

JOB DONE

Computers work faster than you do

Tiredness

Computers never get tired.
Humans get tired after working
for a while.

Computers never get tired

Computers never make mistakes

Mistakes

Computers never make any
mistakes. Humans can make
mistakes at times.

Memory

Computers do not forget any
information stored in them. Humans
may forget the information stored in
their minds.

Computers never forget

Computers do not have feelings

Feelings

Computers do not have any
feelings. Humans have feelings
and these feelings can be
expressed.

Electricity

Computers run on electricity. Humans do not need electricity.

Computers run on electricity

What should I do next?

Computers need instructions

Decisions

A computer cannot make its own decisions. It needs to be instructed. Humans can make their own decisions.

ACTIVITY

Color the features **pink** that belong to humans and **blue** that belong to computers.

WORK FASTER	HAVE FEELINGS
NEED INSTRUCTIONS	GET TIRED
FORGET INFORMATION	NEED ELECTRICITY

Types of computers

There are different types of computers for different purposes.

Desktop

A desktop is a large computer which is kept on a desk. All the basic parts are attached with the help of wires.

Desktops are kept in one place. They cannot be carried from one place to another for work.

Laptop

Laptop

A laptop is a small computer that can easily fit on your lap. You can carry a laptop from one place to another. It is wireless. It works with the help of batteries that can be charged with electricity.

Tablet

Tablet

A tablet is a mobile computer which is very easy to use. It is even smaller than a laptop and can fit in your hand. It works with touch-screen technology and has a keyboard built inside it.

All these computers are called PCs. PC stands for **Personal Computer**. A personal computer is made in such a way that it can be used by only one person at a time.

FACT FILE

Some mobile phones can perform the functions of a computer. They are called smartphones.

Uses of computers

Computers are very helpful in our day-to-day life. They are used in many places to make our work easier and faster.

Schools

Computers are used in schools for many purposes. They are used for maintaining student records, sharing information (time-tables, circulars, etc.) and teaching purposes. Computers are also used for creating report cards.

school

TRY THIS

Computers are also used in libraries. Find out how.

Homes

home

You can use computers at home to read books, play games, watch movies and listen to music. You can even store some important information like phone numbers, addresses and birthdays.

Offices

In offices, computers are used for typing and printing documents. They are also used for sending messages by email. Computers can also store a lot of information which would otherwise occupy a lot of space.

office

Shops and supermarkets

Computers help to maintain records of daily sales and items available. They are also used for printing bills.

shop

bank

Banks

Computers are used in banks for many purposes. They are used for storing customer details. Computers also help to make online transactions. They provide information to the users. Computers are also used for taking money out of the bank at the ATM. ATM stands for **Automated Teller Machine**.

ATM

Hospitals

Computers can be used for storing records of patients in hospitals. They help to detect and monitor diseases. They are used for preparing reports. They help in performing operations and other medical procedures.

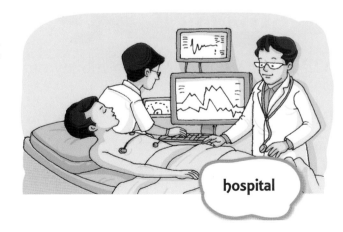

hospital

Railway stations and airports

Computers help with booking air tickets and train tickets. They provide us with information about the arrival and departure times of aeroplanes and trains.

railway station and airport

making films

Making films

Computers are used for making movies and cartoons, and for adding special effects and animations to them.

GLOSSARY

ATM A machine for taking money out of a bank. ATM stands for 'Automated Teller Machine'.

Desktop A computer which is kept on a desk, owing to its size.

Laptop A small computer that can easily fit on your lap.

Personal computers (PCs) Computers that can be used by one person at a time.

Tablet A touch-based mobile computer.

YOU ARE HERE

3

1. A computer works at a very high speed.
2. A computer never gets tired.
3. A computer does not make any mistakes.
4. A computer does not forget any information saved on it.
5. Computers do not have feelings like humans.
6. A computer runs on electricity.
7. Computers cannot make their own decisions like humans.
8. A computer helps in maintaining daily records.
9. Computers are used at many places such as schools, homes, offices, shops and supermarkets, banks, hospitals, railway stations and airports and also formaking films.

EXERCISE

A. **Fill in the blanks.**

1. Humans have made a machine called a ....

2. ATM stands for ....

3. A computer never gets ....

4. PC stands for ....

5. A computer that can be kept on your lap is called a ....

B. Match the names with the pictures.

1. •   • a. Laptop

2. •   • b. Tablet

3. •   • c. Desktop

C. Circle the correct option.

1. A laptop **can/cannot** fit in your palm.

2. **Computers/Humans** can never make mistakes.

3. A computer **does not get/gets** tired easily.

4. A computer **can/cannot** take its own decisions.

5. A desktop computer runs on **battery/electricity**.

6. Computers **do not/do** have feelings.

D. Color the activities green that you can do using a computer.

Checking the arrival time of a train	Planting trees
Creating an animated movie	Withdrawing money
Walking	Playing games

LAB WORK

Illustrate the differences between humans and computers using Paint.

1. Four things that computers can do and humans cannot.

   a. ....

   b. ....

   c. ....

   d. ....

2. Four things that humans can do but computers cannot.

   a. ....

   b. ....

   c. ....

   d. ....

3. Four places where computers are useful.

   a. ....

   b. ....

   c. ....

   d. ....

PROJECT WORK

Interview 5 people (parents, siblings, grandparents, friends and neighbours) around you to find out what they use a computer for. Combine the list with members of your group to make a sheet about uses of the computer.

WHO AM I?

I was born on 23 June 1925 in Shillong, India.

I am known as the Scottish inventor who developed the ATM cash machine.

At first, I was working on the idea of a chocolate bar dispenser. Later I replaced chocolates with money.

I am ……………………………..

The Keyboard and the Mouse

4

SNAP RECAP

1. Find 'QWERTY' on the keyboard.
2. Guess why some keyboards are called 'QWERTY keyboards'.

LEARNING OBJECTIVES

You will learn about:
- different keys on a keyboard
- mouse functions such as clicking, double-clicking, dragging and dropping

The keyboard and computer mouse are input devices. They are used for performing different functions.

The keys on a keyboard

Most keyboards have 104 keys. You have already learnt that a keyboard has Letter keys, Number keys, Arrow keys and Special keys. You will now learn about other keys on a keyboard.

FACT FILE

The longest word that can be typed using only the first row of the keyboard is 'TYPEWRITER'.

Symbol keys

These keys are for special signs and symbols. Some Symbol keys are to the right of the Letter keys, such as /, :, ", >, <, and so on.

Symbol keys

The special characters are also placed over the numbers on the Number keys, for example !, @, #, $, %, *. You can use these as Symbol keys by pressing the Shift key along with the Number key.

Number keys that also serve as symbol keys

Function keys

There are 12 Function keys from F1 to F12 on the top of the keyboard. Each key has a different function to perform.

These keys can act as shortcuts. For example, pressing F5 in an Internet browser will refresh the web page.

Function keys

Shift key

The Shift key is used with the other keys for different purposes.

Shift key

If you press and hold the Shift key along with a Letter key, it will type that letter in capital even when the Caps Lock key is turned off.

For example, [SHIFT] + [A] gives A (when the Caps Lock is off).

Also, [SHIFT] + [A] gives a (when the Caps Lock is on).

There are some keys on the keyboard that have two symbols or a number and a symbol on them.

To type the upper symbol you need to press and hold the Shift key along with the particular Symbol key or Number key.

For example, [SHIFT] + [!/1] gives ! and [SHIFT] + [+/=] gives +

Tab key

You can press the Tab key to move the cursor several spaces forward at once.

Tab key

Escape key

Escape key

The short form on the Escape key is **Esc**. It is placed at the upper-left corner on most keyboards. This key allows you to cancel an operation.

The computer mouse and its functions

Along with the keyboard, if you also learn how to use a computer mouse, then working on a computer will become easier.

You will now learn about the different functions of the mouse.

Clicking

Clicking means the pressing and releasing of the mouse buttons. It is done after pointing at an item.

Press and release the mouse button

Click

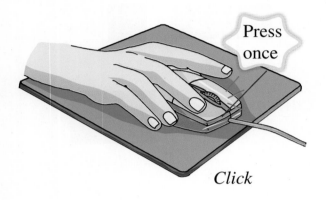

Press once

Click

Single-click

Releasing the left mouse button after pressing it once is called single-click.
A single-click is for selecting an item.

Double-click

Releasing the left mouse button after pressing it twice quickly is called double-click. A double-click opens the selected item.

Click
Click

Right click: to press the right button of the mouse.

Click

Right click

Releasing the right mouse button after pressing it once, is called right-click. It displays a list of properties of the selected item.

Drag and drop

Drag and drop means to select an item and move it to another location on the computer. Follow the steps given below to drag and drop an item.

1. Move and bring the mouse pointer to the item which you want to move.

2. Click on it to select.

3. Press and hold the left button of the mouse.

4. Pull the item to the desired location (Drag).

5. Release the button (Drop).

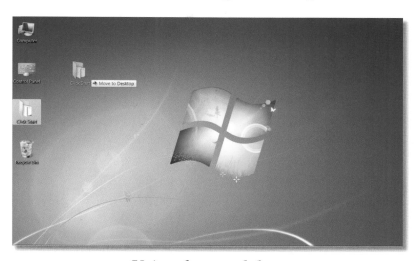

Using drag and drop

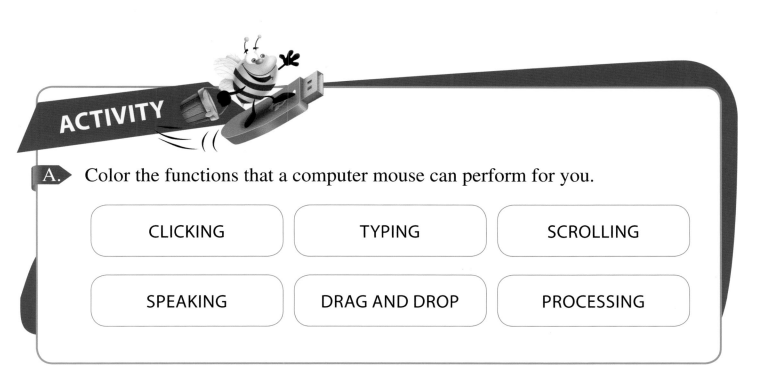

ACTIVITY

A. Color the functions that a computer mouse can perform for you.

CLICKING	TYPING	SCROLLING
SPEAKING	DRAG AND DROP	PROCESSING

B. Find the following words in the grid below.

FUNCTION   TAB   ESCAPE   SYMBOL   SHIFT   NUMERIC   LETTER

F	O	E	S	C	A	P	E
U	Z	S	H	I	F	T	Y
N	C	Y	D	L	J	H	C
C	S	M	W	F	O	D	M
T	A	B	Q	G	W	K	M
I	I	O	Y	C	B	V	N
O	K	L	E	T	T	E	R
N	U	M	E	R	I	C	T

GLOSSARY

Clicking   Pressing and releasing the mouse button to make the computer do some work.

Double-click   Pressing the left mouse button twice quickly, before releasing it.

Drag and drop   Selecting and pulling an item to change its location on the screen.

Escape key   The key used to cancel an operation.

Function keys   Each of these keys has a different job to perform. They can act as shortcuts.

Right-click   Pressing the right mouse button once before releasing it.

Shift key   Used with the other keys for different purposes.

Single-click   Pressing the left mouse button once before releasing it.

Symbol keys   The keys that have special signs and symbols on them.

Tab key   The key that moves the cursor several spaces forward at once.

1. A keyboard has many keys. Apart from those you have already learned about, there are the Symbol keys, Function keys, the Shift key, the Tab key and the Escape key.

2. Clicking is always done after pointing the mouse pointer at an item.

3. Single-click is used for selections.

4. Double-click opens the selected item.

5. Right-click displays properties of the selected item.

6. Drag is to pull the selected item to the desired location and Drop is to release the button.

EXERCISE

A. True or false?

1. There are 104 Function keys on the keyboard.

2. You can press the Tab key to move the cursor several spaces forward at once.

3. Left-click displays a list of properties of the selected item.

4. The Escape key cancels an operation.

5. Clicking means to select an item and move it to another location on the computer.

B. Identify the key.

1. The key found at the upper-left corner on most keyboards.

   ………………………………… .

2. The key used with other keys for different purposes.

   ………………………………… .

3. Keys for special signs and symbols.

   ………………………………… .

4. The key which is used to move the cursor several spaces forward at once.

   ………………………………… .

C. Fill in the blanks.

1. When the Caps Lock is on, [SHIFT] + [A] gives ……………. .

2. [SHIFT] + [! 1] gives ……………. .

3. [SHIFT] + [$ 4] gives ……………. .

4. When the Caps Lock is off, [SHIFT] + [A] gives ……………. .

D. Color the correct answer for each action of the mouse.

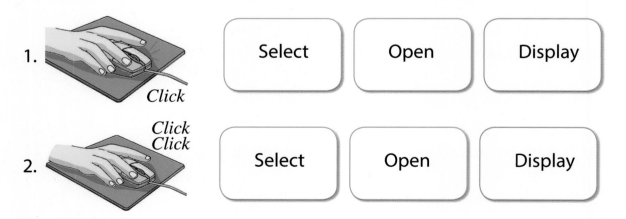

1. *Click* [Select] [Open] [Display]

2. *Click Click* [Select] [Open] [Display]

3.

Click

Select   Open   Display

E. **Answer the following questions.**

1. What is the function of the Tab key?

....

2. What is drag and drop?

....

3. Give five examples of symbol keys.

....

4. What do we mean by clicking?

....

5. Where is the Escape key found on the keyboard?

....

LAB WORK

A. Draw a rectangle and use it to show the position of the Symbol and Function keys on the keyboard.

B. Point the mouse to the Recycle Bin icon on the desktop. Drag and drop it to a new location on the desktop.

PROJECT WORK

Help another student in your class to explore the keyboard, by giving them simple tasks to do. See the examples below.

1. Type your full name with capital letters for both your first name and last name.

2. Type a question.

WHO AM I?

I was born on 14 February 1819.

I am the co-inventor of the typewriter.

I designed the arrangement of characters on a QWERTY keyboard in 1868.

I am ....

Fun with Paint

SNAP RECAP

Use different tools in Paint, for example Pencil, Eraser, Line, Oval, Rectangle and Fill with color, to draw a Thank You card for your teacher.

LEARNING OBJECTIVES

You will learn about:
- starting Paint
- using different Paint tools
- opening a new window in Paint
- saving a picture in Paint
- opening a saved picture in Paint
- closing Paint

Use your pencil and eraser to complete the picture.

You can draw and color a
picture on a computer too,
using a program called **Paint**.

FACT FILE

Paint was formerly
known as Paintbrush.

How to start Paint

Follow these steps to start Paint.

1. Click on the **Start** button on your desktop.
2. Select **All Programs**.
3. Click on **Accessories**. A list of options opens up.
4. Click on the **Paint** option.

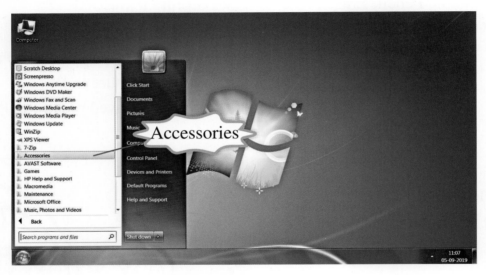

Opening Accessories

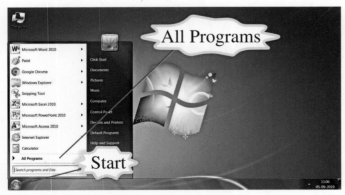

Select All Programs

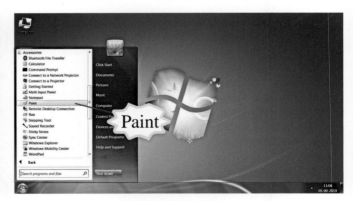

Opening Paint

After following all the steps, the Paint window will appear.

Components of the Paint window

The main components of the Paint window are shown below.

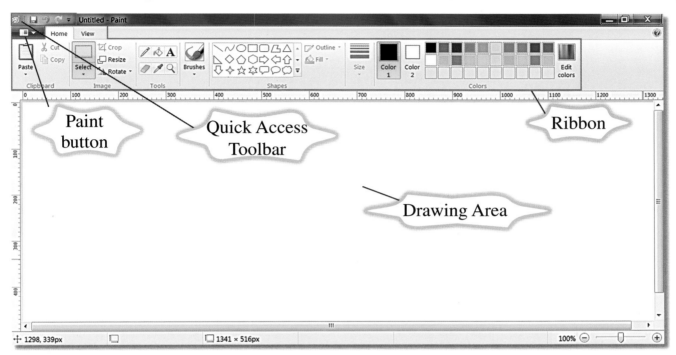

Paint window

You will now learn about these components.

Ribbon

The Ribbon shows different drawing tools. Tabs in the Ribbon are sub-divided into groups. For example, the **Home** tab contains the following groups: **Clipboard**, **Image**, **Tools**, **Shapes** and **Colors**.

You may choose a tool from any of these groups to draw, edit and color your picture.

Paint button

When you click the Paint button, a list of options open up.

Quick Access Toolbar

The Quick Access Toolbar is found above the Ribbon. It is used to access the tools quickly.

Drawing Area

You draw and edit pictures in the Drawing Area.

Using the tools in Paint

There are many tools in the **Tools** group. Different tools are used in Paint for performing different functions. A tool is selected by clicking the left mouse button on the desired icon.

FACT FILE

When you open the Paint window the **Home** tab is opened by default.

You will now learn about some of the tools.

Pencil Tool

The Pencil tool is used for drawing freehand. It is used in the same way that you would use a real pencil to draw.

1. Open the **Paint** window.
2. Click on the **Pencil** tool in the **Tools** group of the **Home** tab.
3. Choose the thickness of the pencil from the **Size** drop-down list.
4. Take the mouse pointer to the **Drawing Area**.
5. Click and drag the mouse to draw.

You can also choose the color of the pencil from the **Colors palette** in the **Home** tab.

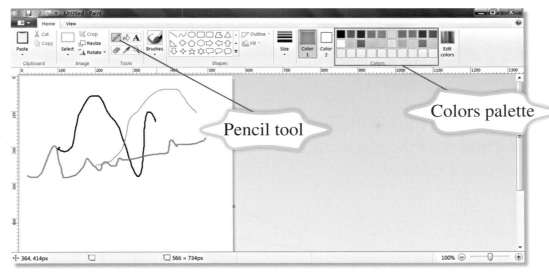

Using the Pencil tool

Eraser tool

The Eraser tool is used for erasing any part of a picture.

1. Open the **Paint** window. Draw a few simple figures and color them.

2. Click on the **Eraser** tool in the **Tools** group of the **Home** tab.

3. Choose the size of the eraser from the **Size** drop-down list.

4. Move the mouse pointer to the **Drawing Area**. A small square appears in the **Drawing Area**.

5. Click and drag the mouse over the part that you wish to erase.

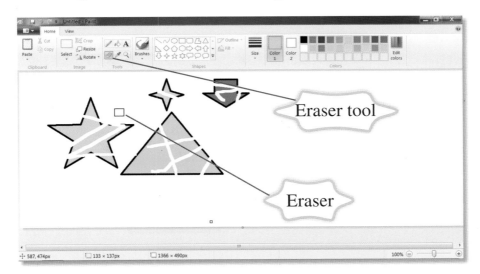

Using the Eraser tool

Draw this picture using the Pencil
tool in Paint. Use the Eraser tool
if you make a mistake.

Fill with Color tool

The Fill with Color tool is used for filling any closed shape that has
already been drawn with a selected color.

1. To color your picture, click on the **Fill with color** tool in the **Tools**
   group of the **Home** tab.

2. Select a color from the **Colors** palette in the **Home** tab.

3. Move the mouse pointer to the area that you want to color.
   Click once to
   fill it with the
   color area.

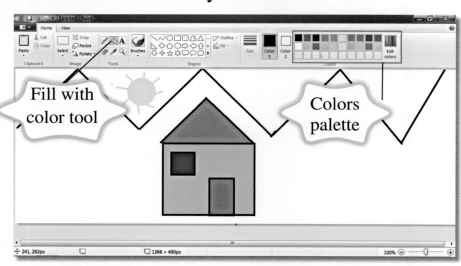

Using the Fill with color tool

Magnifier tool

The Magnifier tool is used to see the drawing at a larger size.

1. To see your drawing at a larger size, click on the **Magnifier** tool in the **Tools** group of the **Home** tab.

2. Move the mouse pointer to the part of the **Drawing Area** that has to be magnified. A rectangular box appears.

3. Take the rectangular box and click in the area to be magnified. Keep clicking to view the image at a higher magnification.

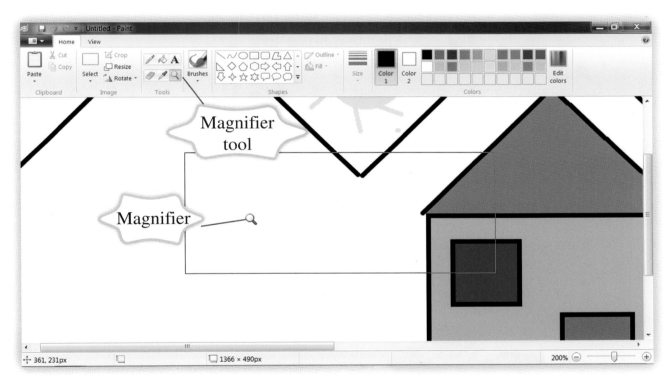

Using the Magnifier tool

Brushes tool

The Brushes tool is used to draw different sorts of lines. You can choose brushes of different textures from the options given to draw free-form and curving lines with different effects.

1. Open the Paint window.

2. In the **Home** tab, click on the **Brushes** drop-down list.

3. Click on the brush style of your choice.

4. Choose the thickness of the brush stroke from the **Size** drop-down list.

5. In the **Colors** palette of the **Home** tab click Color 1, choose a color and then drag the pointer to the **Drawing Area**.

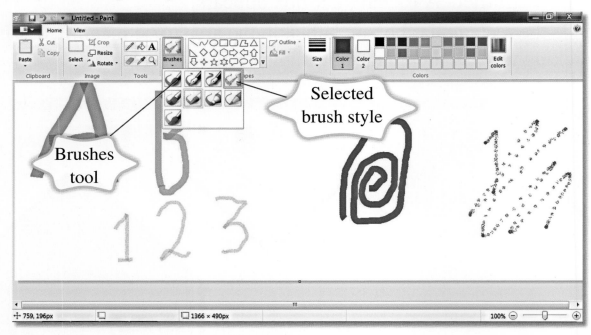

Using the Brushes tool

ACTIVITY

Draw this picture in Paint using the Brushes tool. Then color the picture.

Shapes

In Paint, different shapes are available in the **Shapes** group of the **Home** tab. Here, you can select different shapes such as lines, ovals, rectangles, triangles, lightning bolts, and many more for drawing in the **Drawing Area**.

You will now learn how to use some of the Shape tools.

The Line tool

The Line tool is used for drawing straight lines in **Paint**.

1. Open the **Paint** window.
2. Click on the **Line** tool in the **Shapes** group of the **Home** tab.
3. Move the mouse pointer to the **Drawing Area**.
4. Click and drag the mouse to draw lines.

You can choose the line thickness from the **Size** drop-down list. Choose the line color from the **Colors** palette in the **Home** tab.

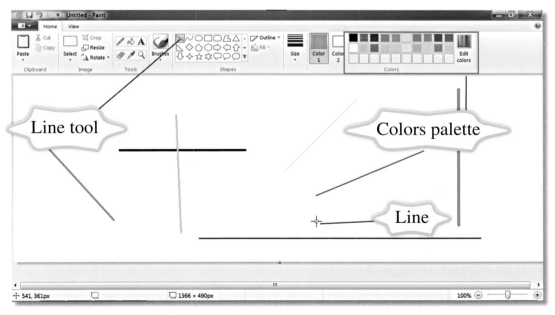

Using the Line tool

Rectangle tool ▢

The Rectangle tool is used for drawing rectangles and squares.

1. Open the **Paint** window.
2. Click on the **Rectangle** tool in the **Shapes** group of the **Home** tab.
3. Take the mouse pointer to the **Drawing Area**.
4. Click and drag the mouse to draw a rectangle or a square.

You can also choose the line thickness of the rectangle from the **Size** drop-down list. Choose the line color from the **Colors** palette in the **Home** tab.

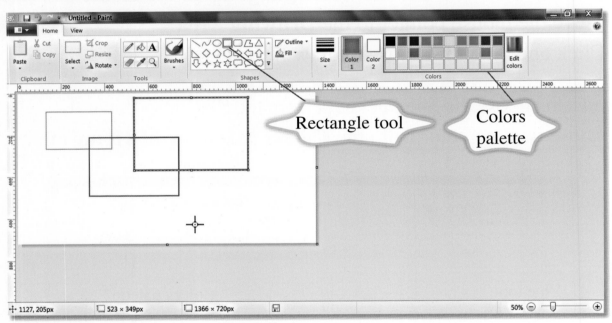

Using the Rectangle tool

Oval tool ◯

The Oval tool is used for drawing circles and ovals.

1. Open the **Paint** window.
2. Click on the **Oval** tool in the **Shapes** group of the **Home** tab.
3. Take the mouse pointer to the **Drawing Area**.
4. Click and drag the mouse to draw a circle or an oval.

You can also choose the line thickness of the circle/oval from the **Size** drop-down list.

Choose the line color from the **Colors** palette in the **Home** tab.

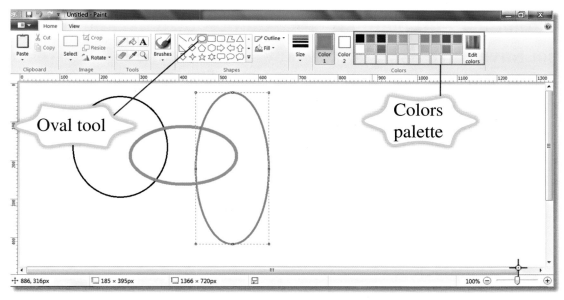

Using the Oval tool

How to open a new window

1. Click on the **Paint** button . A drop-down list appears.
2. Click the **New** option. Your new **Drawing Area** is ready for use.

FACT FILE

Every new picture is called 'Untitled' by default.

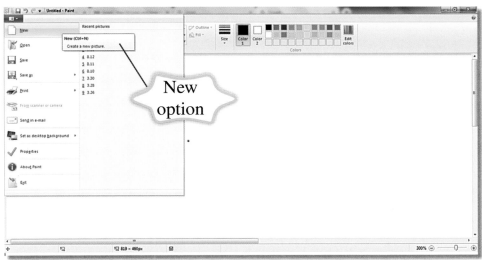

Opening a new window in Paint

53

How to save a picture

You can always save the pictures drawn in Paint. It is good to save the pictures so that you can see them later. Follow these steps to save a picture in Paint.

1. Click on the **Paint** button 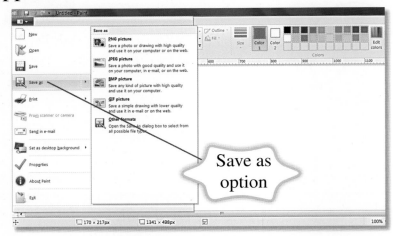. A drop-down list appears.
2. Select **Save/Save as** option. A new window called the **Save As** dialog box appears.

Saving a picture in Paint

3. Type the file name of your choice in the **File name** box.
4. Click on the **Save** button.

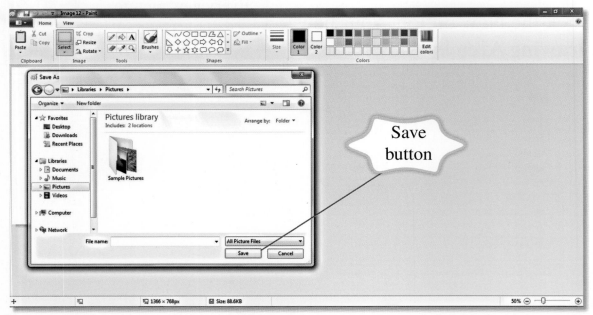

Save As dialog box in Paint

How to open a saved picture

Follow these steps to open an already saved picture.

1. Click the **Paint** button 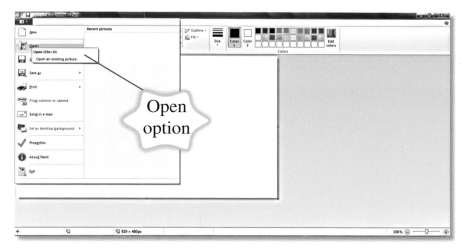. A drop-down list appears.
2. Click the **Open** option. The **Open** dialog box appears.
3. Select the file name from the list.
4. Click on the **Open** button.

Opening a saved picture

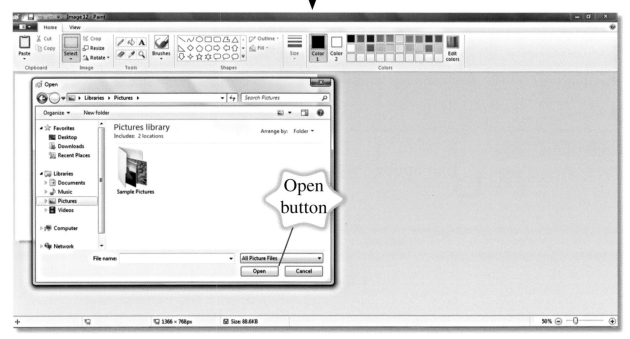

The Open dialog box

How to close Paint

After you have completed your drawing, close the Paint program. To close Paint, follow these steps.

1. Click on the **Paint** button . A drop-down list appears.
2. Click the **Exit** option.

OR

Click on the **Close** button in the upper-right corner of the Paint window. If you have not saved your work, a prompt box appears. Click on the **Save** button to save it.

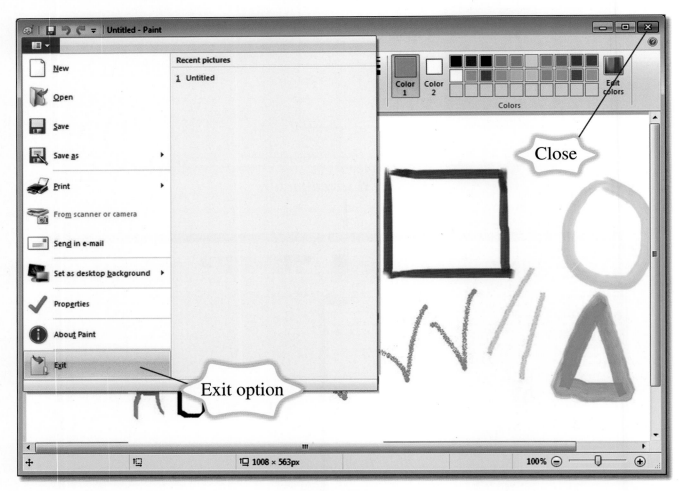

Closing Paint

ACTIVITY

Draw this picture using Paint tools. Color it using the Fill with color tool. Save your picture and exit from Paint.

GLOSSARY

Colors palette The area of the home tab where you can choose different colors for your picture.

Drawing Area The blank area where you can draw and color pictures.

Shapes The different shapes that can be used for drawing.

Tools These are used to perform different functions, such as drawing shapes.

YOU ARE HERE

5

1. To start Paint select:

   Start ⟹ All Programs ⟹ Accessories ⟹ Paint

2. The Home tab has Clipboard, Image, Tools, Colors and Shapes groups.

3. The different tools in the Tools group are Pencil, Eraser, Fill with color, Text box, Color picker, Magnifier and Brushes.

4. The Shapes group contains shapes such as Line, Oval, Rectangle, etc.

5. You can store pictures in Paint using Save/Save as options in the Paint button drop-down list.

6. You can see saved pictures in Paint using the Open option in the Paint button drop-down list.

EXERCISE

A. Tick (✓) the correct tool to draw the following shapes.

1. a. Line ☐   b. Pencil ☐

2. a. Rectangle ☐   b. Oval ☐

3. a. Rectangle ☐   b. Oval ☐

4. a. Line ☐   b. Pencil ☐

B. Correct the following statements.

1. The rectangle tool is used to draw circles.

   ....

2. The Drawing Area is black.

   ....

3. The magnifier tool is used to draw lines.

   ....

4. You cannot re-open saved drawings in Paint.

   ....

C. Label the following picture.

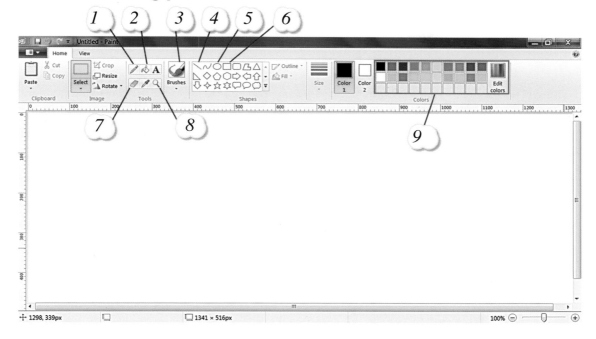

1. .... 2. .... 3. ....

4. .... 5. .... 6. ....

7. .... 8. .... 9. ....

D. Rewrite the jumbled words.

1. EPCINL

2. EASRRE

3. AMGNIREIF

4. SSBURHE

5. NILE

6. ERTCEANLG

E. Answer the following questions.

1. Name the main components of the Paint window.

   ....

2. What is the function of the Eraser tool?

   ....

3. List the steps to open a new window in Paint.

   ....

   ....

4. List the steps to save a picture in Paint.

   ....

   ....

   ....

   ....

LAB WORK 🖥

Spend 5 minutes on your computer, and draw anything that is in your mind using Paint. After 5 minutes, go to the next computer, look at what your neighbour has drawn and add to your image.

Go on until you've visited at least 5 computers. Now, look what you have drawn and save it with a title.

PROJECT WORK

Design a book cover for the book you like reading the most and give it a new title. The image below is an example.

Introduction to MS Word 2010

6

LEARNING OBJECTIVES

You will learn about:

- opening MS Word 2010
- components of MS Word 2010
- creating a document in MS Word 2010
- saving a document in MS Word 2010
- opening a saved document in MS Word 2010
- closing a document in MS Word 2010
- exiting MS Word 2010

Introduction

Microsoft Word (MS Word) is a program that helps you to type words on a computer. This program helps you to write essays, letters, poems and much more. This chapter uses MS Word 2010. For MS Word 2016 updates, go to the end of the chapter.

FACT FILE

Several versions of MS Word are available, such as MS Word 2003, 2007, 2010, 2013, 2016 and 2019.

How to open Microsoft Word 2010

Open a word document by following these steps.

1. Click on the **Start** button on the desktop.
2. Select **All Programs**.

3. Click on the **Microsoft Office** folder.

4. Select **Microsoft Word 2010**.

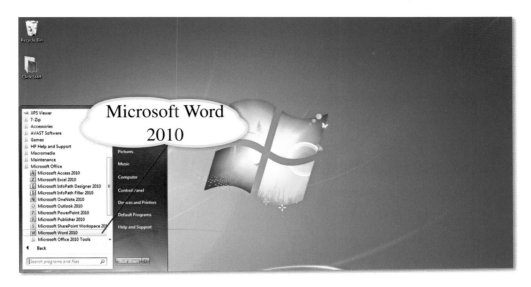

Components of Microsoft Word 2010

After following all the steps, the Microsoft Word 2010 window appears as shown below. You will now learn about the components of MS Word 2010.

FACT FILE

MS Word was formerly known as Multi-Tool Word.

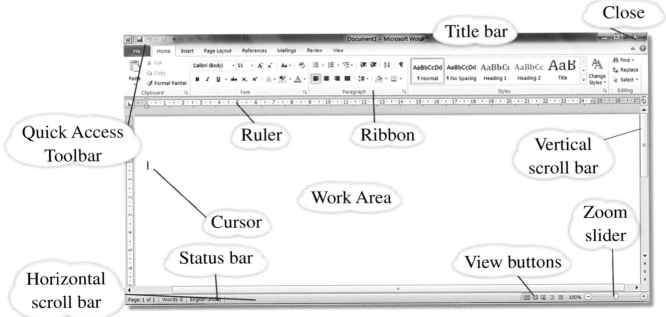

Microsoft Word 2010 window

Quick Access Toolbar

The Quick Access Toolbar appears at the upper-left corner of the MS Word 2010 window.

It contains buttons for commonly used options such as Save, Undo and Redo.

Title bar

The Title bar appears at the top of the MS Word 2010 window. It displays the name of the program and the active document.

Ribbon

The Ribbon appears below the Title bar. It is divided into tabs such as **File**, **Home**, **Insert**, **Page Layout**, **References**, **Mailing**, **Review** and **View**. Each tab has several groups. These groups contain various options used in MS Word 2010.

Ruler

The Ruler measures the length and width, and shows the margins.

Scroll bar

The Scroll bar is a long thin strip with arrows and a sliding section at the edge of the window. There are two scroll bars.

| Horizontal scroll bar | Vertical scroll bar |

Horizontal scroll bar: Used for shifting the screen display left or right.

Vertical scroll bar: Used for shifting the screen display up or down.

Work Area

The Work Area is the area in the document window where you type the text.

Cursor

The Cursor is the blinking vertical line in the Work Area that shows your location.

Status bar

The Status bar displays the page number, word count, language, page layout and zoom slider.

View buttons

MS Word 2010 has view buttons like Print Layout, Full Screen Reading, Web Layout, Outline and Draft. You can view the page on which you are working in any of these formats by just clicking on the buttons directly.

Zoom slider

You can zoom in to get a close-up view of your file or zoom out to see more of the page at a smaller size.

How to create a new document

The steps to create a new document are given below.

1. Click on the **File** tab from the **Ribbon**.
2. Select the **New** option from the left pane.

Creating a new document in MS Word 2010

3. Click the **Blank document** from the templates that appear. A new document opens.

TRY THIS

Press **Ctrl + N** to open a new document.

Every new document has a default name Document1. Each time you open a new document, they will be named as Document2 and so on.

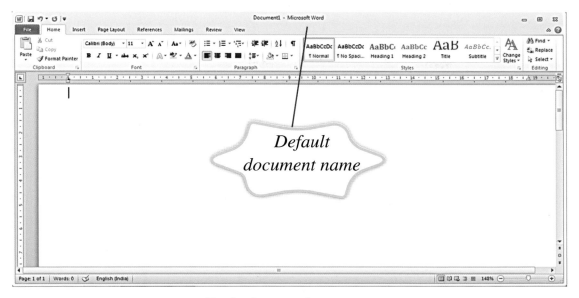

Default new document

MS Word 2010 offers many ready-made templates to choose from.

How to save a document

In order to save your document in a new location, follow the steps given below.

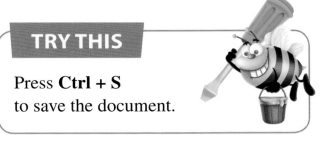

TRY THIS

Press **Ctrl + S** to save the document.

1. Click on the **File** tab from the **Ribbon** and select the **Save/ Save As** option from the drop-down list.

2. Select the location where the file is to be saved in the left pane. Type the name of the file in the **File name** text box.

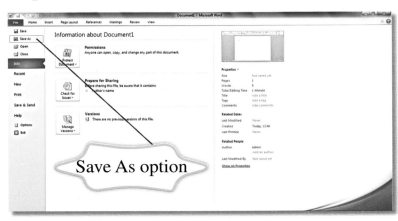

Save As option

3. Click on the **Save** button in the lower-right corner of the dialog box.

Saving a document

Selecting a file location and entering a file name

How to open a saved document

Follow these steps to open a saved document.

1. To open a saved document click on the **Open** option from the **File** tab.

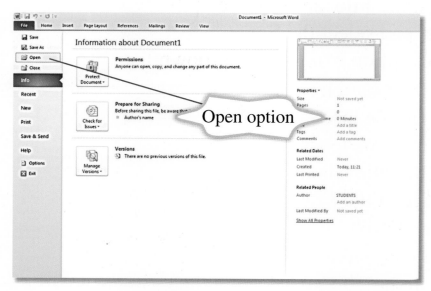

Opening a document

2. Select the file name from the Open dialog box that appears or type the name in the **File name** text box.

TRY THIS

Press **Ctrl + O** to open an existing document.

3. Click on the **Open** button at the lower-right corner of the dialog box.

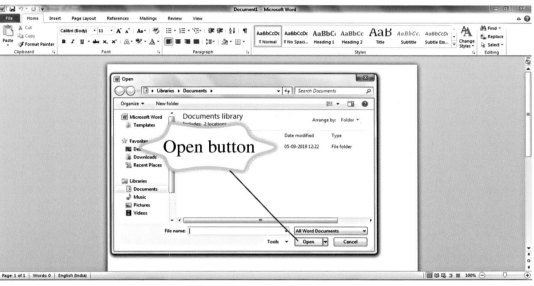

The Open dialog box

4. If you have recently saved a document, click on the **Recent** button. It appears on the list towards the right of the drop-down list. Click on the document to open it.

Opening a recently saved document

How to close a document

To close a document in MS Word 2010, click on the **Close** button in the upper-right corner of the **Title bar**. If the document has not been saved, a prompt box appears. Click on the **Save** button to save the changes.

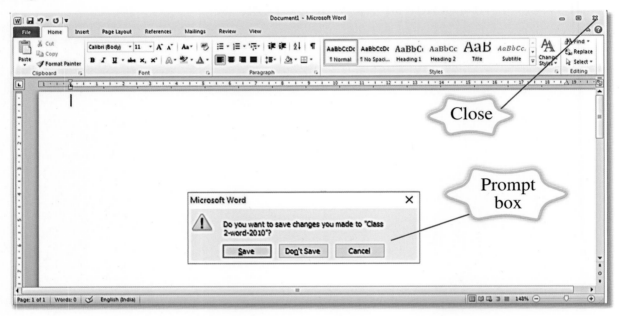

Closing a document in MS Word 2010

1. Click on the **File** tab from the Ribbon and select the **Exit** option from the drop-down list.

2. If the document has not been saved, a prompt box appears. Click on the **Save** button to save the changes.

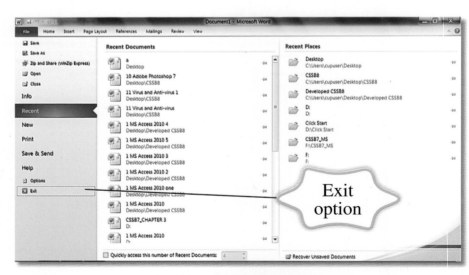

Exiting MS Word 2010

A. Find the following words in the word grid.

Ribbon	Open
File	Word
Cursor	Save
Document	Ruler
Toolbar	Close

X	R	C	U	R	S	O	R
F	I	L	E	G	V	B	P
Q	B	K	C	L	O	S	E
Z	B	J	S	A	V	E	Y
D	O	C	U	M	E	N	T
P	N	H	R	U	L	E	R
W	O	R	D	O	P	E	N
M	T	O	O	L	B	A	R

B. Color the correct answer from the choices given for each question.

1. Open

| File tab | Ribbon | Status bar |

2. Page number

| Ribbon | File tab | Status bar |

3. Name of the file

| File tab | Title bar | Status bar |

4. Save

| File tab | Title bar | Status bar |

5. Word count

| Title bar | Ribbon | Status bar |

GLOSSARY

Cursor The blinking vertical line in the Work Area. It shows the position where a letter, number or symbol can be typed.

Dialog box This box asks for information to be given to the computer.

File tab This tab has options such as Save, Save As, Print, etc.

Horizontal scroll bar Used for shifting the screen display left or right.

Quick Access Toolbar Helps to directly Save, Undo or Redo changes in the Word file while working on it.

Status bar Displays information about the current cursor position.

Title bar Displays the name of the program and the active document.

Vertical scroll bar Used for shifting the screen display up or down.

View buttons Buttons in the status bar like Print Layout, Full Screen Reading, Web Layout, Outline and Draft help in changing the view of the page.

Work Area The area in the document window where you type the text.

YOU ARE HERE

6

1. Microsoft Word is a program where you can type and write essays, letters, poems and much more.

2. To start Microsoft Word 2010 select:

   Start ⟹ All Programs ⟹ Microsoft Office ⟹ Microsoft Word 2010.

3. The different components of MS Word 2010 window are: Title bar, Ribbon, Rulers, Scroll bars, Work Area, Cursor, Status bar, Quick Access Toolbar, and View buttons.

4. You can create a new document in MS Word 2010. Every new document has a default name, Document1, Document2 and so on.

5. The Save and Save As commands are used to store the typed text.

6. If you try to close a document in MS Word 2010 without saving it, a prompt box appears. It reminds you to save it.

EXERCISE

A. Correct the following statements.

1. The Zoom slider measures the length and width of the page in MS Word 2010.

   ....

2. The Title bar consists of buttons for the most commonly used commands.

   ....

3. The vertical Scroll bar is used to shift the screen display to the left or right.

   ....

4. The Quick Access Toolbar displays tabs such as Home, Insert and Page Layout.

   ....

5. The Cursor is the area in the document window where you can type the text.

   ....

6. The Ruler helps you type in Microsoft Word.

   ....

B. Match the following.

1. Title bar •	• a.	Contains multiple tabs like File, Home, etc.
2. Ribbon •	• b.	Blinking vertical line in the work area
3. Quick Access Toolbar •	• c.	Measures the length and width
4. Cursor •	• d.	Displays the name of the program
5. Ruler •	• e.	Contains buttons to Save, Undo and Redo

C. Look at the following picture carefully. Answer the questions that follow.

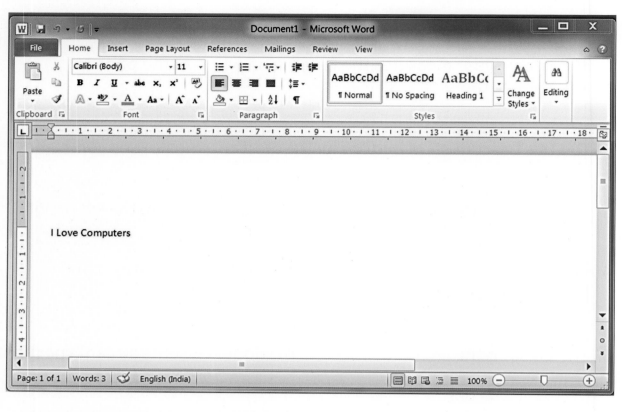

1. What is the word count shown on the Status bar? ....

2. Identify the name of the document from the Title bar.

....

3. What is displayed in the Work Area?

....

D. Answer the following questions.

1. What are the View buttons in MS Word 2010?

....

2. What is the Work Area?

....

3. What are the tabs available in the Ribbon?

....

4. What is the role of the Status bar in MS Word 2010?

....

5. What is the Scroll bar used for?

....

LAB WORK

A. Complete the following exercises in MS Word 2010.
1. Write 5 good points about your best friend.
2. Write 5 lines about your experience of working in MS Word.

B. Save the above documents on the desktop. List the options you see when you save them using the Save As button.

PROJECT WORK

Imagine you are teaching someone to work in MS Word. Write 10 steps/instructions in your notebook about how to work in MS Word.

MS Office 2016
Updates

1. When you open MS Word 2016 for the first time, the Start screen appears. From here, you can create a new document, choose a template or access recently edited documents.

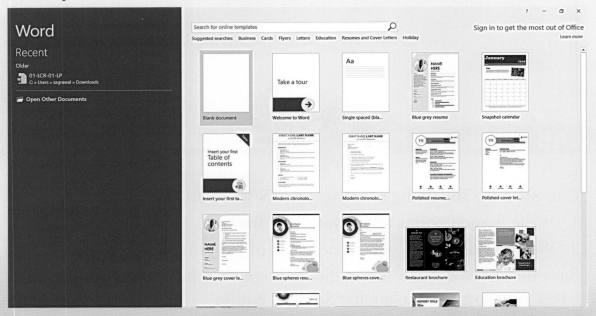

2. The Ribbon of MS Word 2016 looks like this:

Sample Paper

Tick (✓) the correct option.

1. **Identify the printer from the given options.**

    a. ☐   b. ☐   c. ☐   d. ☐

2. **Which key must be used to go to the next line?**

    a. SHIFT ☐   b. ENTER ☐   c. ☐   d. CAPSLOCK ☐

3. **On railways, computers are used for:**

    a. reservations ☐   c. painting ☐
    b. playing games ☐   d. withdrawing money ☐

4. **A CD goes into a CD drive. Where does a USB go?**

    a. Pen drive ☐   c. USB port ☐
    b. Hard disk ☐   d. None of the above ☐

5. **Which of the following tools in Paint is used to erase in your drawing area?**

    a. Pencil tool ☐   c. Fill with Color tool ☐
    b. Eraser tool ☐   d. Text tool ☐

6. **Which device is used to carry files?**

   a. Monitor ☐   c. Printer ☐

   b. CPU ☐   d. Pen drive ☐

7. **Which of the following keys should be pressed with symbol keys to type symbols?**

   a. CTRL ☐   b. ENTER ☐   c. PG DN ☐   d. SHIFT ☐

8. **Identify the device shown in the picture.**

   a. Joystick ☐   c. Light pen ☐

   b. Mouse ☐   d. Keyboard ☐

9. **Identify the Recycle Bin icon.**

   a. ☐   b. ☐   c. ☐   d. ☐

10. **In MS Word 2010, you can open a blank document from ....**

    a. File tab ☐   c. Review tab ☐

    b. Insert tab ☐   d. All of the above ☐

11. **Find the odd one out.**

    a. Right-click ☐   c. Type ☐

    b. Left-click ☐   d. Scroll ☐

12. **A mouse should always be kept on a ....**

    a. Mouse pad ☐   c. Notebook ☐

    b. Table ☐   d. CPU ☐